A Piece of Rope

Kathryn Gosling

Published by New Generation Publishing in 2020
Copyright © Kathryn Gosling 2020

First Edition

ISBN 978-1-80031-674-4

www.newgeneration-publishing.com

New Generation Publishing

For Mum,

Thank you Mum for always liking
anything that your daughter does—
that is one of Mum's jobs after all !

I thank Aunty Gill for keeping the gift of poetry, handed down from
'Nanna', alive in our family. Thank you for all your inspiration and
love, for the hours we have spent enjoying songs and rhymes from
Winnie the Pooh and for all the times we have added our own words!
Ruth for just being there, helping, supporting, and for the bond and
love that is only shared between two sisters.
And I thank my husband Ian for giving me a new start in life and
showing me that love is alive.

Thank you

Dear Friends,

Everyone has a bucket list, it may not be written down on paper but held in your head — these are sometimes known as dreams. It is a list of things you would like to do. This is number 7 on mine, to write a book. I am 56 years old and I have no idea how I got there. I have held on to my rope tightly and have been caught up in the many knots, some good, some bad as I have travelled along it. In 2018 I became a married woman again. I own my house, the first one I have really ever loved with all my 'precious' things around me. In every corner both in and out you will find at least one bear or a bear-related item collected over the years. I also enjoy designing and making my own collectors' bears. I am coming to the point in my life when I feel time is more precious now than a career and recently bought a sundial for our garden to keep reminding me of this decision! I am a sensitive person and anyone who knows me really well - that would be my sister - knows that I need constant love — some say I am high maintenance! Ian says I am his world - with the occasional earthquake. That's me.

Ruth, my sister, my rock - that's it. After losing Rosalind, our younger sister 13 years ago we have stuck together like magnets. Occasionally we get the poles mixed up but that never lasts long. Chris, my brother-in-law is still very much in love with Ruth and together they amble through married life climbing hills and occasional mountains together working it all out. Ruth is very strong and assertive so when things do come to a head Chris just agrees and all is well — a lesson Ian still has to learn!

I am not going to mention my son who now lives with his dad. I am the monster waiting for him to return one day but that is another story.

Aunty Gill is our rock, she emigrated with Uncle Paddy and their family to the land of Oz in the 70s. Technology has increased over the years and with it air travel, meaning we could continue to make more memories as the years move on. I am sure she would come back to us from overseas but with her own children and their families, and now with Paddy's ashes buried there - I guess those are her rocks and there she will stay. We love her to bits, she is a missing part of us and leaves a raw hole.

Mum – we have climbed some mountains and travelled along very rocky roads but she is still Mum and I love her.

Ian is the hand that reached out to me and showed me a different way of living.

There are many others who have touched my life in one way or another as I travelled along and some of the poems I have included reflect on this.

Over the years I have written many poems, all meaning something at the time. They are about someone, something, a feeling or a point that needed to be made. Written on whatever bit of paper I had at the time I decided to try and sort through them and put some of them down on paper for real. I dedicate this book to Mum as she has always listened to a poem and said how good it was just like when a child creates something at school and brings it home to proudly present to 'mum'. She will always give it pride of place on the shelf or eat it with 'Yum, Yum, when are you making some more?' or hang it on the wall where it would eventually end up in her keepsake box for you to rediscover at a later date. Others have read them and said they are good but it can never compare to the praise your mum gives you. My sister also has the gift of poetry when the occasion calls for it but like me she needs to be inspired by a need to write one. We get this from our Nanna, handed down to her daughter Gill, who can also knock up a cracking verse or two when the need arises. The gift of poetry missed Mum! Some of the poems included are self-explanatory and others I have jotted down a note of introduction.

So here is a collection that seems to tell the story of my life better than an autobiography could. They show my feelings, some humorous some sad, offer words of comfort and some tell stories that needed to be heard. I hope that somewhere along the lines you will connect with one of them, find comfort in those that offer support or think of a friend who needs a hug.

Happy reading
Kathryn

Contents

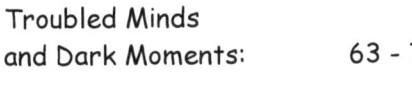

My Own Piece Of Rope
Let me introduce myself ....

A new life starts, a new story begins,
Many pages there's no guarantee
And things that happen along the way
Will mould this person into me.
At centre stage, *all* family around
(though changes do take place)
The memories held deep within
Keep a smile upon my face.

My world expands, two sisters join
And all the years that follow
Hold memories and cherished moments
Some chapters threaded with sorrow.
Like snooker balls we'd fire off
In different directions we'd slide
Innocence and emotions take over
As on life's roller-coaster we ride.

Dark moments are always woven
Into each of life's gold thread
One parent leaves, 'tis another's story
Memories are left in a young girl's head

My first love I'd plan to marry
For he was the world to me
My uncle on feet I'd forever travel,
My eyes no one else would they see.
At that age who could argue
When his turn for love came around?
How shattered was I, heartbroken,
Now grown, a new friend I've found.

For some School Years are quite the best
But for others a dark lonely place
Demons around each corner
Demons you're destined to face.

Nanna moves in bringing sunlight
A house of girls now rule
Now we're older, we miss her so
Hindsight can be so cruel.

At 21 bells brightly announce
A new chapter that will begin.
If only I'd listen as they rung out
Oblivious to troubles they bring.
Tommy comes to share our life
For my dog, a chapter I'd write
A move is made, a son is born,
The future seemed so bright.

People are such funny creatures
It's the animal world for me
I feel more at home with them
For they love you unconditionally.
Birds of prey and chipmunks,
Chinchillas, a duck and Tommy
A rescued fox, magpie and owls -
We soon had a complex menagerie
People who know me can see a thread
Woven tightly into each knot
A love, a friend, a passion, a need,
Bears will always mean a lot.

Life can be cruel and unexpected
Our sister we fought with when young,
Her pages are full, her story too short,

Leaving two now acting as one.
Years pass, another time to grieve
Tommy leaves me with heartaches galore
Sam joins and becomes my saviour
With love and devotion he opens a new door.

Family is everything and another story ends
Taken from across the world's seas
Our love is stronger than miles it seems
Together the sorrow we try to ease.

My rope becomes a noose,
It thickens every day
Drags heavy and weighs you down
It's hard to shout out and say.
Mental scars leave a shell
Living an emotion that's new
A rocky road to travel, a struggle to move on
Like tar, divorce is hard to pull through.
It's a deep well that isolates and
Quicksand that pulls you down
Emotions are raw, try to take stock
Rest awhile with new friends found.

A son is a gold thread that's woven
Deep inside your veins
Care, love, experience, support
Given by a mum whose energy drains.
With his own story to write, you pray soon
He'll understand the reasons and fight-
The past which is gone, and reconnect
And on my pages once again write.

Suddenly a light ahead
As warmth now fills the air
A man who shows that love's alive
And we soon become a pair.
I never thought true happiness
Was something that I'd own
It always seemed for others
For me always seemed on loan.

A new chapter has now started,
With pages all clean and bright
A wonderful home, a dream to fulfil,
Each tunnel does have its light.
As this new journey starts another two end
'Tis the way of each life string
Two daughters and husbands, Mum's partner now gone
- and Sam, old age is a terrible thing.

Every journey needs friends who care
Be they close or wider apart
No story can ever be complete
Without friends who have touched your heart.
For those through my life who have added their strand
Special friends at work I am counting
I thank you each and every one
For you helped me climb each mountain.

Jobs over the years have changed
As I developed into who I am
From office to animal, people to children
Who knows of His great plan?
Now just a number on a pay role?
But for 19 years I did bring
Knowledge and skill, the hours I'd spend
To this school I gave my everything.

As I think of this chapter I'm now living in
I'll climb mountains - and boulders I'll move
It's now time to enjoy, to plan on ahead,
And dark memories to remove.
So here I sit, my story goes on
Starring friends, relations and family
Uncles and Aunts, Nephews and In Laws
My Sister, my Mum, my Husband and me.
X

Family
Pages 11 - 20

The gift of love is often wished
At special times of the year
So many cards are signed 'with love'
Some may bring a tear.
But one is blessed with happiness
When you're with loved ones dear
For the real gift is family
And having them always near.

Mum, my sister and her husband flew to Australia for a holiday with Aunty Gill and Uncle Paddy. I could not go this time so I sent a solar light with them to complete the family gathering.

I Shine For You

As the day grows old and the sunlight goes down
Drinking on the patio, my light will shine around.
As the light dims more, the wine will flow
The laughter will ring out for this I know.
This little light of mine will shine and shine and shine.

You are all near throughout the day
But our family wasn't complete until the day faded away
For this little light of mine
Will complete us – let it shine.

Outside as you sit in the dim moonlight
I will be there, though silent, through the night
And when the breeze comes and the living room does call
Take me inside with you for I'm the light in the ball.

I love you all and miss you so
So close are we, but this you know
Gill, our verse, our ties so strong
Paddy, cherished memories live on and on.

My sister, my friend I love so much
Mum, I miss your warm tender touch
('tis more than one alone can bear)
So this little light of mine
Please let it shine and shine and shine.

Gill's plane ride home following one of her visits.
Ruth and I gave her a card to open on the plane.

Flying High

We know you're flying high right now
We know just how you feel
'cus we've just spent three months with you
(or as much as we could steal)
We've more times to talk about
And more memories to keep
And other precious moments
For both of us to reap.

We love to have you to ourselves
And will joke to achieve
But you are one and there's two of us
So you've twice as much to receive!
And so we'll both continue
To look forward to the day
When we are all together again
So start saving again – OK!

We will also try real hard
And start our savings too
In order to be together again
This we promise you.
During your stay with us
We were both flying high
So full of love and happiness
So hard to say goodbye.
Though miles may be many
We'll sing a different tune
For it won't be long
Our love's too strong
We'll see you again real soon.

The Big Three 0

You can always spot a woman
Who has reached the Big Three 0
The sagging bum and drooping boobs
And wrinkles may start to show!
Don't worry, don't fret, don't get upset
Everything will be just fine
You can still look good each day –
- it just takes a little more time!

The fellas still look, some may pass,
Don't worry too much anymore
The fellas that stay are usually the ones
That offer all you could ever ask for.
You're not missing anything really,
You've gained an awful lot
Experience and Maturity
Now add to what you've got!

Seriously, this is it,
The fun will start I know
And if you don't have laughs galore
There's always the Big Four 0!
So wake up bright and early,
Look in the mirror – what do you see?
A stranger staring back at you?
– face it girl you look like me!

The Christmas Wish

As we've all grown older
We've stopped giving gifts
That we chose each Christmas
From some very long lists!

But it's not nice to get *nothing*
At this special time of year
(Although I now don't dread
The credit card bill with fear!)

Being together is wonderful
With lots of food (drinks too!)
But I really wanted to give you something
Just from me to you

I know to give a bear
Would be a laughing joke
And you don't want chocolates
As do some other folk

You do not want jewellery
Or some fine bath pearls
And you're not into fashion accessories
Like some of the other girls

And I couldn't *wrap* a gift up
That just wouldn't seem right
When we'd decided not to -
I'd have to keep it out of sight!

So I give you my penny
'*What for?*' I hear you say
'Tis to pay for the wish
You make this Christmas Day

The Birthday Gift

Happy birthday dear sister
With lots and lots of love
A day out together
Is what I'm thinking of
I'll drive on over
And stay the night
Play cards and drink,
All sounds just right.
Then we'd wake,
And by car or train
Travel somewhere
That you will name
We'll wander around
Have lunch for two
Shopping? Maybe,
Just me and you
Then home we'd go
After a wonderful day
Although dear sister
There is something I must say
For really in truth
I'm a little selfish you see
- being with you
is really a gift for me.

A Precious Thing
for Ruth

Love is only four small letters
Some say the strongest word around
But there is one far stronger
And more powerful I have found.

If love is as precious as gold
And diamonds all sparkling and bright
Then SISTER is Rhodium and Platinum
Both rare and a beautiful sight.

If you're looking for unique and most valuable
Jade and antimatter are the very top two
But records are a bit out of date
Because they haven't discovered you.

To have someone that's part of you
Who knows secrets they don't tell
It's not a husband or very close friend
Or someone who knows you well.

It's someone connected by an invisible thread
Unbreakable no matter how long
Like carbon and titanium
No force could be as strong.

We can tell each other anything
And keep it locked away
It only brings us closer
Having a part of the other each day.

The Sound of Silence

Raucous Roz

Our sister is amazing,
A fact that you all know
And Roz is very special
Right from head to toe~
Precious in so many ways
But one stands back a mile
When she opens up her mouth
For anything but a smile!
Her very special quality
I'm sure you'd all agree
Is more something that you'd hear
Not so much you'd see!
Her looks are quite stunning
A fact that's very true
And when she's all grown up
She'll turn a head or two
We all have a voice
Of that there is no doubt
But she has the sort
That kinda stands right out!
Her voice is quite fantastic
The tone it reaches far
Her sopranos and saxophones
Can be heard wherever you are!
A life without our sister
(although the sound we may forfeit)
Would never be the same
'cus we love her every bit!

The Last Word

Oh my dear sister, now you really should know
You think you've had the last word?
Well that's not the way it will go.
I remember many nights together
We've laughed, we've loved, we've cried
We've also fought like cat and dog
('though promised Mum we really tried)
We have so many memories
That we both deeply share
Bringing us closer together
Showing how much we care.
I know you're angry deep within
I know you feel you're right
I also know in life's great plan
It's not worth this stupid fight.
We only have a little time
In God's great plan for us
So let's hug and make up
And stop this great big fuss.
We are both tied together
Not just by blood and birth
For that's just string unwound
And can reached anywhere on earth.
Our tie is made of rubber
Wrapped with silver and gold
It keeps us close together
As together we grow old.
If we go up against each other
Neither would really win
For we know too much of the other
And neither would give in!

We take strength from each other
You are my core, my rock
I couldn't bear to be without you
That would be too much of a shock.
So stop this silly argument
Life's too short to miss
Let's make this The Last Word
'cus I'm your big sis!

Friendship
Pages 21 – 28

As you travel along your own road you'll never travel alone
True friends are always there in person, or at the end of a phone
We don't very often tell them and we really should say more
Celebrate them and let them know their friendship you're thankful for.
BUT
There's *so many* poems out there answering 'What Is A Friend?'
Thousands of words will tell you the qualities they commend
So I'm *not* going to pen about humans, now don't get me wrong
For my friends are all a godsend (as in poems mentioned further on)
I'm going to give a shout out (bet you can guess can't you!)
To those silent friends who lend a paw and forever *bear* with you.

(A footnote to the animal world:
Some pets are simply unique and If you're lucky enough
To have shared a life, no truer companion you'll meet)

The Forgotten Bear

There are lots of bears
In this old world
Famous bears
Who've made their name
But don't forget
The one you're holding
Has special love
Just the same
He may not be famous
Nor well-dressed
He may not look
Quite his best
But has as much to give
As those famous few
And all his love
Is just for you

Bear Parts

The moment I saw you
you touched my heart
And I now understand
why I was given each part
My legs are to follow you
wherever you go
My arms are to hold you
and love you so
My stuffing to soak up
the love that you give
My heart to be yours
for as long as you live
My ears are to listen
My eyes are to see
My mouth is sealed
which was meant to be.
Each part of me was made
With care and thought
And now I'm with you
I shall love you
Just as I've been taught.

Waiting Patiently

It's you
I know it
I've been waiting you see,
Sat on this table waiting patiently
I knew it was you – I saw you across the room
I tried to shout you, hoped you come soon
And now that you're here I've so much to say
NO WAIT – don't go - please stay.
I need you to know that there's more to see
Look beyond my coat and discover my personality.
I know that there's lots to choose from today
I hope I'll find someone special who'll stay.

I'm still sat here, still waiting patiently
Sat here for what seems an eternity.
And now it's the end of the day,
And I didn't get my chance to play
I'll wait till next time, that's what I'll do
I'm picked up to pack – No wait -*it's you!*
I didn't think you had noticed me at all
As you looked at others on the stall
Do you want a cuddle? I've plenty to give
I'll give them all to you for as long as you live
You want me to listen? I'll not say a word
I'll keep very quiet as though a word I've not heard.
And I'll keep the secrets that we two will share
For as long as you need me I'll always be there.

My Old Teddy

Brownie was given with love as old as time
From my granny in Norfolk and he was all mine.
He was my birthday present and was as big as me
I was just 2 years old - there was no one as special as he.
I grew and watched him wear with love, each night on my bed he'd be
And though I'm much much older now, he still lives a life of Riley.
A pram was bought in which he'd go for rides all dressed in white
Never quite sure of gender, he always behaved just right!
As time wore on and years did pass Brownie was still true
A loyal friend, a secret shared, he listened and advised on what I
should do.

Married now and he's still here, watching me grow older
He's stories to tell should he wish and still he lends a shoulder.
I remember times when he was hung dripping from large round ears
He's patchy now with worn-out fur from my love over the years.
Son your power rangers, who've all come and gone
Did they listen, stay with you? Did they? – No not one.
Let me remind you when young of a special friend
Be-Bop was your bunny. For you the rules do bend?
I caught you talking softly to him and asking some advice
You tell me you're too old now but I've caught you more than twice!

So don't roll your eyes and shake your head
When other bears do come
To take their place upon my bed
Beside Brownie – My number one.

A Friend For Life
Winnie The Pooh

You'll love the sound of your mother's voice
And in your memory you'll keep
Her soft and gentle rhythm,
As she lulls you off to sleep.
In later years you'll listen
~ Just before you go to bed
You'll remember her rhythm and tone
As the stories are repeatedly read.
His loyal friends you'll all soon love
And get to know so well
A favourite you'll soon discover
As you learn to read from cover to cover!
Through teenage years, when times seem tough
And you feel there's no one there,
Turn a page and read a poem
They'll remind you of those who care
And when you later find true love -
Smile and proudly say,
That you're a fan of Edward Bear
He'll love more that day!
The children you will later 'bear'
Will love your voice so sweet
And tears will fill your eyes
As you recall stories from memories deep.
In later years that follow
As grandchildren come to play
Introduce the Wonderful World
Of Winnie the Pooh (a bit each day!)

And if you grow to love him as I do
You'll find that day by day
You'll quote, think or laugh about
A line or poem that he'd say.
Find comfort and words of wisdom
Treasure his book as years move on
May you share in the joy and happiness
And enjoy his journeys one by one!

Sorry

I have a special friend
Who means a lot to me
But something made me sad
As I found out recently.
For a Birthday was celebrated
- They happen every year!
But this one was a special one
And it brought me to a tear.
To think I had forgotten
And missed the change to say
'You're one in a million
for you I'm grateful every day'
Everyone has birthdays
But not everyone is you
For you are very special
These kind of friends are few.

Stories To Think About
Pages 29 – 46

Stories have always been told
Since the beginning of time
By word of mouth or on pages
Short or long and those in rhyme.
Some teach, some just for pleasure
Soothingly read when afraid
Some warn of dangers and troubles
Others have a point that needs to be made.

The Fairy Door

For Mum

Love is very precious
A priceless gift to give
It's free, yet can be hard to find
In this troubled world we live.

It's often not said enough
To those who mean so much
Although it's always there
In each warm and tender touch.

Now wouldn't it be lovely
If the fairies got things done?
Or the pixies and the leprechauns
With their mischief and fun!

The chance of a fairy door
And asking them to call
A small and priceless gift of love
Yet the biggest gift of all.

For it's not just anyone
That the fairies travel to
It's only someone special
Who's loved as much as you.

So I arranged with fairyland
(I'm sure you'll find a space)
For you to own a fairy door
A portal to an enchanted place.

Through their magic door
Amongst the plants that grow
They'll bring my love when I'm not there
As they freely come and go.

My House

I love my house, it's lived in, I've 'clutter' everywhere
Magazines left open, things left on a chair.
Kitchen worktop covered, the conservatory you can't see
There's only one person who likes it and that one person is ME.

But friends they keep a calling, 'A Wonderland' they say
Nick Nacs around every corner amongst the strands of hay.
Chinchillas in the dining room, fish in the hall
Careful in the conservatory or over the duck you'd fall
Every room is a mystery, on every shelf a find
A house of clutter maybe but the animals don't mind!
Come find a chair and sit awhile, listen to the sound
Pick up a bear (they're everywhere)
Relax and look around.
If you need a whats-a-ma call-it,
Or are short of a thingy or two
If I haven't got one handy then I'll make one for you!
I live a funny life but be sure of one thing
A host of entertainment and amazement I bring.
The only thing now on my mind – bear with me I know it's late,
If people keep a calling
How much should I charge them at the gate?

Mum and I went to London for the day.
Mum has always been known for her ability to plan
trips and holidays to the max, to include everything
that she considered *needed* to be seen!

A Day Out In London

A day trip to London, the reason was to see
The Phantom of the Opera (not a first for me)
We decided to take it 'easy' and so with map in hand
You planned a dash around, just missing out the Strand.
First Oxford, Regent and Baker Street
Then the London Eye was seen
A dash back to the tube station
For Harrods' bear department (my dream)
For the bear that was sought
This shop just couldn't be missed
And a visit to their wine department
Soon saw us drunk!
With airs and graces we tried the lot
The tasting was a treat
It gave us a new lease of life
And put us back on our feet.
This being the case we started again
- pressies to be got
And if we'd had any more wine then
We'd have bought the ruddy lot!
A meal was planned before the show
Steak and wine the treat
But running out of time now
Mc D was the place to eat
And so with bags and bags (and bear)
We sat on our theatre seat
Then walked to catch the coach back home
With happy heart and aching feet!

Miss You

for Gill and Paddy

Travelled to town, wandered around
Saw Winnie The Pooh and thought of you
Went on holiday, just to get away
And what did I do? – I thought of you

Garden Centre pots full of Forget-Me-Nots
- honest it's true – I thought of you
Rocking in my chair, into space I stare
Glass of wine (or two)
Thinking of you

Not a day goes by when I don't glance at the sky
And guess what I do – I think of you.
So my days are filled, my night times too
What I'm trying to say is 'I Miss You'

The world is so big, can't swim, can't dig
Wish the miles were few.
I'm thinking of you.
It's now winter overseas
(poor Paddy would freeze)
But I'm warmed through with thoughts of you

Sitting here writing,
Tears I'm fighting
Feeling blue
Sweet thoughts of you.

One holiday Paddy commented on the number of
'silly ol' moos' that he saw over here and 'yet more sheep'
he'd see in almost every field! For a number of years
gifts revolved around the two. Until a poem was sent
- from you know who!

Cows and Sheep

I travel to work, I shop sometimes
And everywhere I turn you know what I find?
They stare at me, they haunt my night
I now dream in black and white.
There are pens, pencils, pots
And of T-towels there are lots
Paper, pads, they just don't care
Displayed quite proudly everywhere.
Not just in shops but on my way to work
Behind the hedges they all lurk.
Some may claim after a drink or two
~They see pink elephants (which is what I used to do!)
'Pigs might fly' once used to be heard
But now they're replaced with a large white herd.
It's almost enough to turn ewe T-Total
Situation desperate, situation fatal.
And now it's winter and guess what's around
Damn woolly jumpers ten to the pound
And when it's time to go to sleep
You know what I count? Those bloody sheep!
So take one last look and enjoy what you see
For these are the last you'll get from me!

The Drinks Mat

Morning...
If the mat is full, leave it be
If the mat is empty I'll have a tea.

Eleven's...
Visitors arrive, here we go
Can have one early to be sociable you know

Afternoon ...
One o'clock, two, three, four
We're nearly there – tea no more.

Tea Time...
It's almost time when I'll be sat
With glass in hand and an empty mat!

Evening...
It's not that I've been waiting for this time of day
But now it's here Hic Hic hooray!

Supper...
One more for the road then it's time for bed
Don't need no rocking
Night night sleepy head.

The School

A School is made of a tough outer shell
But it takes more than bricks to support it well
A place to send your kids each day -
Teaching children is just 'child's play'
And what about all those holidays galore?
Staff spend relaxing on a Sunny shore.
Teachers there 9 to 3.30 - and breaks too!
What a cushy job. If only you knew!

For it's not just standing at the front of the class
Following the curriculum our Government passed
True, some staff do leave at the end of the day
While others have work and have to stay
Planning, preparation, teaching and testing
Clearing away, marking, re-planning and assessing
Wiping noses, tending to knees
Policing playgrounds we all do with ease
Politicians, social workers, listeners all feature
Angels, clowns, jugglers, friends – (oh and teacher!)
Progressing the children along the way
Coaching social and life skills throughout the day,
And all of this following 'health and safety'
The paperwork alone is enough to drive you crazy!
Homework – sent home for children to do?
Did you know teachers and TA's do it too?
Every evening and through half term breaks
I can't tell you the hours that this all takes.
And all the meetings we must attend
Ironing out issues, problems to mend
Some staff have additional tasks covering
Subject co-ordinating and all the ordering

You also have TA's that are further qualified
Who do all this *plus* they guide
Those who have a special or challenging need
Specialising in helping them to succeed
Then there are clubs that some staff run
Sparking interest, enjoyment and fun
Covering a range of different activities
All planned for the many different abilities.
Office staff make up our strong back bone
Sorting parents, paperwork and calls on the phone
At lunch time the dinner ladies then rule -
Yet another essential team for the school.
Then there's the ladies who cook all the dinners
Warm smiles, healthy food - they're all our winners
And the playground - just a place to run around?
No a team of play leaders will be found.
And when children are gone, the cleaners clean
For it's not the fairies that make everything gleam!
Heading this team is our friendly Caretaker
Equipment mender and building maintainer
Governors watching everything done
Their job to oversee and support everyone.
We help each child and watch as they grow
Gently guiding them in the right way to go.
No two days are ever the same
In this 'cushy' job some think a game
The hurdles we leap and mountains we climb
Our senses are all on overtime!
We may all suffer from total exhaustion
But we think our job is totally awesome.

Little Gems

C is for the cuddles that they give to you
H is for the happiness and the heartaches too
I is for the interesting things that they do
L is for the love they give to you
D is for the little darlings for that's what they are
R is for the rights and wrongs they have learned so far
E is for the energy, they seem to have so much!
N is for the number of things since our lives they touched.

The Memory Book

Our life is filled with moments when
Warm feelings and smiles take place
And once they're past we can forget
As our mind may in time erase.

Our story is filled with precious times
We really shouldn't forget
Something we heard that made us smile
Memories can fade like sunset.

People who touch our lives
Weave a thread of golden chain
Years soon pass and time moves on
A moment we'll never see again.

If we could only make a note
That would never fade away
A memory book of moments
Or things that loved ones say.

So scribble a note, a thought or two
A photo frozen in time
To ensure you don't forget and bring
Those memories back to mind.

The New Arrival

Since we first found out and shared in all your joy
We've been wondering if it's a girl or boy
And now we're at the end of this guessing game
We still need to wait to be told her name!

My sniggering through your sickness
The wonderful reason I knew
(I found it quite amusing
for me that is, not you!)

But as you journey into motherhood
Each day you seem to glow more –
Enjoy each precious moment
Don't listen to tales of what's in store!

Her life will be so full
Of the love that you both share
Such tenderness and devotion
There's nothing can compare.

So from one friend to another
And of course to daddy too
I wish you love and happiness
Can't wait to meet her (and of course see you!)

Creams for Wrinkles

All birthdays are special
But milestones are few
They give us cause for celebrations
With drinks and parties too.
Now any age is worrying
Should you stop and think
Cards with 'gentle' reminders
Could drive some to drink.
Creams for wrinkles
Creams with collagen
Creams to make you young
The companies have you hooked
Once you have begun.
Of all the creams that you can buy
(And there are quite a few)
How many do exactly
What they say they'll do?
The best medicine for your skin
To liven and refresh?
It's not the products they tell us to buy
Try laughter and love to beautify!

Adopt A Bear
October 2018

These bears all lonely and forlorn
From a charity shop once loved, now worn
Their purpose very clear to see -
Were for the bride's planned Hen Party.
Liane, my friend who loves me dear
Created the whole atmosphere
Crafts before we sat to dine
Then naughty games and lots of wine!
Jane my other 'right-hand man'
Had her own organised plan
Photos she took captured memories made
Both special friends and both a bridesmaid.
Lots of fun - we had a ball!
Bride and Bears enjoyed it all.
My problem now, (if you know me)
Is very plain and clear to see,
A large group of bears, or 'Sleuth' is what
An Arctophile (that's me) has got
With different bears in every room
Our house is like a museum!
Ian hopes you'll take them one by one
Until all bears are 'safely gone'!
Love him, keep him safe and 'Reuse'!
(Or 'her' should a bride you chose)
Just pick your bear and on their tag
Write your name (My husband will be <u>very</u> glad!)
Then take home your adopted bear
And give them all your love and care.

The Colours of War

Pink then white
Red then black
Leaving blue
Sorrows stack

Healthy then shock
Blood and despair
Sadness and grief
Everywhere

Life so happy
Then on one command
Fear takes over
Red fills the land

Black remains
For those new gone
We sing, we hear
Their victory song

The colours of a story
Forever told
Forever fought
Brave and bold

Empty helmets
War condemn
For us, our future
Remember them

THE BOGGART

Have you ever lost anything? Put something down and it has mysteriously 'gone'? Then you may have a boggart problem – you'd best read on!

OK, where did you put it?

Put what my dear?

I KNOW it was you

I have no idea!

What? Someone just came in? As quiet as you please?
Yesterday my brush, and NOW my keys
I went for my coat, left the keys on that chair -
And when I returned THEY JUST WEREN'T THERE

Don't be silly dear, your mind has been tricked
They probably fell under the chair and were kicked.

Now I know you're playing 'cus it's happened before -
Oh what's the next thing you have in store?

A long time ago I was once told,
About creatures that live, all creepy and bold
They run through the house, sniggering and unkind
Moving things around, playing tricks on your mind

OK where did you put them? I know it was you,
Trying to scare me with things that you do.

They can be wrinkly, old and have no hair
They decorate themselves with things moved from
here to there
You don't know they've been but you suddenly find
Something lost or missing - and you think it's
your mind!

Please stop your fun for you're scaring me
If it really wasn't you then who could it be?
Wait - did you hear anything then? It is quiet tonight
I glimpsed a sweeping shadow, it's given me a fright.
An awful feeling, all creepy and cold
Like something watching you, fear taking hold
In that shadow – something green and brown
Twisted and gnarled with a swishing sound

Oh dear, it sounds like a Boggart to me
The culprit I speak of you'll never see!
A Boggart's a creature all gnarly and old
They disguise themselves, many tales have been told

A household spirit living in woodlands and clearings
Causing mischief and mayhem with things disappearing
They're quick, they're fast, they run through your house
They're smart, cunning and as quiet as a mouse
So lock all your doors, don't let them inside
For they'll always find places to sneak and hide
Be careful if you have one - they're not all the same
Some are nasty little blighters and play more than a game
Next time you lose something or think it's misplaced
Watch for that shadow - past your window it raced
You can't get rid of them once they take hold
They'll stay for good – never do as they're told
Tales have been passed down over the years
Of their mischief, fun and their love to cause fears
You must never give them a name, unless you want them to stay!
For with your mind he will surely play!

Now – where are those keys?

A Heroic and Marvellous Wedding Night
Helpful Advice for a Groom!

I've been thinking of something helpful to say
And have a few things, some advice if I may.
It's just a few guidelines for when you 'hit the sack'
Don't act like Rambo on account of your back.
007's got the gadgets (you'd have to improvise)
And Schwarzenegger's got the body but let's not fantasize
Steed's a true gentleman now that you can be
But she'll be looking for something spicy, daring and raunchy
Don't be too adventurous, you're not Super Ted
Just don't try to rush things, you've only just got wed.
Danger Mouse is out – health and safety you know
Green Turtles and Deputy Dog – those areas and all NO GO.

That Lone Ranger disguise just wouldn't be quite right
Nor Mr Ed or Muffin (they'll be no horse'n around tonight)
You could be Flash Gordon but I think that slow is best
You've got to be Bionic Man and be better than the rest!
Don't be a Dare Devil, play it safe and plan
And unless you can make the Earth Move that cuts out playing
Superman!
Don't bother with X Men or Batman 'cus you haven't got any wings
So you can't jump off wardrobes or do other silly things.

The Fantastic Four is out – the problem you may ask?
To do four things at once you'd have to multitask.
Thor, God of Thunder used his weapon well
But by the time you've read all this – She'll be too tired to tell
There's lots more Marvel-lous men who could all inspire you
My advice – leave it to the female sex -
They always know what to do!

46

Ecology Stories
To Ponder Upon
Pages 47 – 52

Under the weight of our progress
Under the heat of the sun
Under the light of the moon and stars
Our Earth she struggles on.
Stop for just a moment
Take note of what you see
Think about the future we're changing
Take in her natural beauty.

The Polar Bear

The Past – What is it?
A memory to behold
For bears that lived then
Didn't get chance to grow old.

The present – that's us
You and me.
Can we really change
And create new history?

The Future – Bright?
Will your grandchildren see
Those mighty bears
That once lived free?

Mountain Rivers
an Indian Tale

As strong as the mountain with head held high
As wise as the rivers that run beneath sky,
He sighs oh so heavily, his stance true and strong
He gazes at his names sake and wonders what went wrong?

Yesterday, though younger then and as far as the eye could see
He played amongst each blade of grass and in rivers running free.
Today he gazes over the land, the grass is not so green
His sight now blocked by a different mountain, one like he's never seen.

This concrete monster is not new, it's raised its head before
Spears and arrows cannot compete for they will only build more.
Such beauty that this land once had, that taught his people well
Some will never see, others too blind, just whose was it to sell?

'Why?' he asks the mighty sun as down his spine he shivers
He takes one last look at his own namesake
Mighty Mountain Rivers

A Petal Falls

A thing of beauty to gaze up,
A symbol of hope and peace
'Tis another gift from Mother Earth
Her wonders never cease.
A delicate petal falls
Like a tear drop on the land
Why can't people see
And fail to understand?
Such disregard we show our Earth,
We torture her and suffocate
How long will she support us
If we continue at this rate?
We need to be more thoughtful,
Change our ways and think ahead
Don't throw that rubbish in the bin
Reuse, Recycle, Reduce instead!

Shine Bright

A reminder to be Green through and through
Let your light shine in everything you do.

For it takes just one to shine and people will then know
They will all see quite clearly the right way to go.

Just one bright light and people will see
That is doesn't take much to be Eco-friendly.

You are that one light and with the glow that you give
People will see the right way to live.

So keep shining brightly as you travel your road
And teach all you meet your own Eco Code.

A Greener Plan

Our ABC's our 1- 2- 3's, things we all should know,
Our Earth needs looking after too we don't want it to go.
Our friends our school our family - we all love to see,
Our Earth is also special, just like you and me.

Lots of smoke and rubbish too, cutting down our trees.
Wasting water, lights left on, listen to me please
The weather's getting warmer now, the ice is melting fast.
Lots and lots of wind and rain - how long can it last?

Walk, eat fruit and drink a lot, care for all our plants
Animals need our help too – from elephants to ants!
These little things we all can do - just look at what we've got
If we work together now we can help a lot.

I will try my very best and think about what I do
Be ECO friendly at home and school and make a difference too
Let's Re-cycle every day,
Reduce our rubbish in some small way
Re-use it if you can,
And let's all follow a Greener Plan.

Supporting Poems
Pages 53 – 62

No one can do it alone
Days can be heavy and long
Hard to stay above water
Hard to stay focussed and strong
Some look to the heavens above
For strength when a loved one is gone
Or at a time when you feel lonely
-We also have friends to lean upon.

An Angel, A Friend

Some say they are heavenly
And dressed all in white
Some say they are mystical
And a wonderful sight
An Angel is an advocate,
A light that may be seen
Maybe just a wish
Or a person on whom to lean
Your Angel may take many forms,
Sent from heaven above
They touch your life in some small way
Bringing peace, joy and love.

Not many are so fortunate
To have this special gift
To touch a person's life just once
And give a needed lift.
Should this ever happen to you
Along life's dusty road
Then thank the Lord for giving
A true friend to halve your load.

Distance

Everything I see
Everything I do
Everything all through the day
Bring loving thoughts of you.

I see a happy smile
I feel a warm embrace
And deep inside my mind
I can see your loving face.

I hear a silly song
I think of tunes we share
Don't ever not believe
How much I really care.

I may not phone each day
To let you know I care
Or be able to fly away
And be with you over there.

But I am with you always
Constantly from head to toe
My love is in the sun's warm rays
(I think you really know).

And should your day cloud over
And a cool breeze touches you
On your own you're never
'Cus I think the world of you.

Our brain is a wonderful thing
Without thinking we do what we do
And while I continue my daily routine
My thoughts are still with you.

Thinking of you is easy
I do it most of the time
It's like eating chocolate
      Or big cream buns
           Or supping a glass of wine!

Don't Forget You

Our lives are touched by many things
Most good, some bad it's true
The bad can seem so very big
And can really affect you.
A hurtful word or something seen,
Not recognised for who you are
Can all affect the way we feel
And change our day by far.
It takes a special person
To keep your head held high
And continue to be positive
As the days slip by.
A special kind of person
Of those there are so few
And it's time for a reminder
That one of those is you.
You're one in a million
(I think I've said before)
And I'm not the only one
Who will give you a 'top score'.
So when you look at others
Just remember who you are
You're the one they wish they were
That wonderful shining star.

Love In A Difficult Time

With love you climbed each mountain
And made it to the top.
With love you tackled problems
That never seemed to stop.

With love you made the memories
You keep to this day.
With love you'll hold them close
As you continue on your way.

For continue you must
Each day is one that's new
You are the rock that stands
And family look to you.

You must be strong, not bend
Under each heavy load you bear
Gain strength from all that love you hold
And remember -
you have friends who care.

In Times Of Need

Just when you feel it's over
And you really can't go on
Just one knock too many
And your energy has gone
When you sit and ask the question
And you think of what's been done
'How can someone do this
for it really isn't fun'
After you ask yourself why
And shed a tear or two
Considered your options –
A light comes shining through.
Gentle hands are offered,
Pick you up and point the way
Put you on your feet again
Tomorrow's a brand new day.
So never give up hope
For there *are* people who care
Who will always give support
And will always be there.

No Words Can Say

I know this time is special
In a sad sort of way
Although you're not alone
I just wanted to say
I'm thinking of you always
They say that time does heal
I have been through this too
And I know how you feel.

I've looked at hundreds of cards
Where hundreds of verses spoke true
Each verse had hundreds of words
But none were right for you.
Sending love through words
Are all nice to read
But words can never give
The hugs that we need.

I've looked through the dictionary
The thesaurus too
And in two hundred thousand words
None were right for you.
So I've arranged with the sun
To show you there's a light
Don't slip into the dark
The moon shines bright tonight.

The gentle breeze that blows
Soft against your cheeks
Let it remind you I am here
As days turn into weeks

You will get through this I know
You may travel a rocky road
Please never ever forget
You have me to share the load.
A foggy journey ahead
But the days will start to clear
With love from friends and family
And having them always near.

A Pillar To Lean On

for M

There is a time in life for everything
To live, to love, to die
Some are taken to soon
Leaving us a time to cry.

In troubled times we often see
Things we do not understand
Our boat it can rock with uncertainty and fear
Until on solid ground, again we land.

For some they're left with holes
Although they may not show
Deep inside there's an empty space
Where dark waters still flow.

This time is unforgiving
Waters swirling all around
With nothing to hold on to
One can get weighed down.

We are your pillar of strength
For our roots are solid and strong
Made of family and our friendship with you
Always there when needed for however long.

We'll support you, we're here for you
We'll give you the strength to go on
It won't repair the hole you have
But it gives you a pillar to lean on.

Troubled Minds
And
Dark Moments
Pages 63 – 70

Sometimes we stumble and fall
It can be hard to get through each day
You pray the light at the end of the tunnel
Isn't another train heading your way.

Stay Safe

Covid 19

Stay safe my precious family,
You're everything to me
I'd climb mountains, swim oceans
Break rules to be there
At your side whenever needs be.

Stay safe my relatives near and far
Though often we may not meet
You helped to make roots I need to grow –
You are the strength around my feet.

Stay safe my friends I need you,
Just to know you're there
For I know I seldom show or tell
You're part of my life's story, and I care.

Keep safe for those who need you
Keep strong and don't give in
Keep going
Keep positive
Keep fighting
Keep smiling
Keep hope alive within.

The Last Resort

Don't get stressed out –
Leave work behind
(and those who cause it)
Relax and unwind.

Take a week off work,
Have a holiday, eat and drink
And look at ways to eliminate
That stress related link.

Some swear by square breathing,
It depends on how you use it
And of course where, in your place of work
It would blooming well fit!

Take a little chocolate
That usually works just fine
But if you find you're needing more
Then take a little wine.

Yoyos are a good release
(I've heard it said somewhere)
Never really tried them
And quite frankly I don't care.

Stress putty is always fun
You can squeeze it and pretend
It's someone's head or arm or throat
Or sometimes your best friend!

As a last resort if you're still stressed
And not having any fun
Then eliminate the problem
And use a bloody Gun!

The Heartbreak Of Mother's Day

Mother's Day is a time to show
That she's everything to you
Without her you wouldn't be here
Living life to the full.

She gave you all the time she had
There was nothing she wouldn't do
Took you places, played your games
She lived her life for you.

But for some this day brings heartache
Sadness and despair
For those who are no longer with us
Or have sons that just don't care.

5 Balls

We all juggle 5 balls unknowingly, some master it quite quick
For some it takes a while before the correct rhythms click.
It can take a lifetime to learn this art of juggling balls
And if not balanced correctly, all but one will fall.
5 balls don't seem too many, but in everyone's life they'll be
Work and friendships, love, health and family.
Work is the largest, growing heavy at times it's dropped
Made of rubber it just bounces back
This cycle must be stopped.
The other balls are precious and made of glass they'll crack
If dropped too many times they'll smash and not come back.
These balls are very fragile, they will break, they need care
Let them drop too many times and they will no longer be there.
Don't let work rule your world it will soon become foggy and stain,
Guilt and stress become your norm as only work will remain.
Once fallen into that dark lonely pit with sides too steep to climb
It's hard to break out into fresh air again
And clear your troubled mind.
You need steps building to help you out, you need those glass balls
    that slipped
You need to change the balance of the scales the work ball tipped.
Words are your friends, they'll help you, once out they're seen,
You must make that climb and change the way you've always been.
Inside is a wonderful person weighed down by the mask you wear
The heavy chains you carry and the boulders and rocks you bear.
So help me to break this cycle, help me to break free
Give me the steps, the ladder I need
For inside this body is me.

I Feel, I Am

I have been touched by stars, there *were* times when I think
But now I'm at a junction again, trying not to sink.

Swirling waters all around throwing me from side to side
Filling my head, my lungs, myself with nowhere safe to hide.
And then deep inside a mountain with rocks and stones on top
Each heavy with a memory I wish to God I'd forgot.

Everyone has knots along their own life string
Each knot a memory or milestone and with them emotions they bring.
It's hard to try and talk, to express this mould that grows
People think you're happy and your life it gently flows.

You've tried to let words out but you're afraid they might see
The different person trapped inside this body that is me.
To others you are successful, bright, clever and knowledgeable
Full of common sense, able to help anyone else in trouble.

The fear that I have is to open up inside
Tell others that I'm struggling, my brain cells are fried
Electricity moving so fast, drink numbs the pain at times
Just can't seem to think, just sit avoiding more land mines.

I have so much, so why this angry feeling within?
Pull yourself together, sort yourself out and start living.
So much around me, so clever I am, I have no need for this
I need to stop it, move on, cut away the mould and let it be gone.

 But I don't say anything for fear it will bring
Another boulder on top which may topple
everything.

The Question Of Love
The Human Workout

Just what is it? Someone please tell
On this subject we'll all question and dwell.
You could love sport, you can love bikes and cars
Surfing the internet, gazing at stars
You can love animals, chocolate, a glass of wine
Music, a book, a simple touch or family time.
Can you separate love? Know when it's real?
From things to people to emotions you feel?
A chance you take? Or a gamble? A dream?
Sharing life with someone, becoming a team -
Part of their world, now known as 'We'
Thinking of them *all* the time – no more I and Me.

For if you live as one, missing the little things that matter
Raw emotions like a raging waterfall will invade and shatter.
You wait for that someone, that touch, those kisses,
Who completes you, gives you oxygen, you change to Mr and Mrs
No matter how far along in your life's chapter
Everybody wants to live Happily Ever After
Knowing, respecting, protecting, understanding a soul mate
Together you'll find a way, manage any heavy weight
At times you'll sit and question and one thinks that they know best
While the other backs away - is it really a stupid test?
And who decides who passes? Or suddenly draws the curtain?
A simple gesture? Is that enough? Or is the future uncertain?

How long is your elastic, will it eventually snap?
Too far, too fast, too long and it will just widen
the gap

One step away is one step too many for each minute, each day
Each hour it takes they'll just be further away
Then one will just turn and close the door
Too far the distance and they *won't* be hurt anymore.
So re-think those thoughts that run through your head
And think about actions towards a body that's already bled

Love is a workout for body and soul
Are you thinking single or part of a whole?
Do you find quicksand or a future of concrete?
Mend the gap and build solid ground to meet?
Learn about who you live with, know who they are
Love can either be unconditional or leave damage, a raw scar.

Death

Pages 71 - 76

Death – the final chapter
The end of a person's rope
For those left standing and grieving
It can be a slippery slope
Stand firm with family and friends around
Stay strong for there is hope
For they left you with memories to keep
And love to help you cope.

Time

There is a time in life to love
A time to laugh and cry
A time to say you're sorry
And a time to die.

There's a time to be born
A time when dreams will fly
A future for you to plan
And a time for you to die.

Time is such a fleeting thing
The moments too soon fly by
Years float away like seeds on the breeze
Too soon the time to die.

A 'lifetime' promises many things
But a lifetime is a lie
Too soon when you find your path
It seems it's time to die

Time to call on memories
We made along the way
As we remember loved ones
Who came to the end of their day.

Some are taken quickly
To soon in life to die
Leaving a hole for those who grieve
It's hard to say goodbye.

And now your time has come
As we gently wipe an eye
For you now sleep with those we love
It's time to say goodbye.

Rosalind (08.07.71 - 25.04.07)

from Kathryn and Ruth

Three young girls we grew together
Tumbling through the days
Laughing, crying, fighting, sighing
Travelling separate ways.

We faced life's rocky challenges
We took them all head on
We just didn't get enough time
To finish your full life's song.

Though your time so short
Your precious days so few
We shared laughter and love,
We fought and cried
As all good sisters do.

The love and cherished memories
The times both good and bad
Years we've lost
We can never get back
Nor bank the time we had.

We'll never know of God's great plan
Or why this had to be
Our feelings now
So sad, so lost
God's plan is hard to see.
We'll cherish the life we shared with you
Now fate has weaved her spell
As we three are now just two
With a little less to tell.

And so dear sister if you can hear
These words we send to you
You will always be a part of us
In everything we do.

Smiles, laughter, sorrow, tears
Leave memories of too few years
Deepest thoughts forever keep
Now drift with dolphins, and gently sleep.

.

Tommy
(13.02.87 – 03.05.02)

Tommy you were once a sight of which to tell
But over the years age did work her spell
How wrong can I be, how cruel that I am
For yesterday a small pup, today an old man.
Curled up in my arms you travelled home with me
A handsome little chap and two became we three
Intelligence I remember and for granted I took
The understanding face and the all-knowing look.
You gave me everything, nothing did you hide
For every time I needed you, you were always by my side.
So many happy memories of days spent with you
So many times you'd make us laugh with things that you'd do.
My belly stared swelling 'get rid the dog' they'd say
You proved a caring companion as another came to stay.
For Ben you were a playmate, you watched him as he grew
Your true thoughts and feelings – if only we knew!
And now you rest your soft brown head silently on my knee
Those same big brown eyes gazing up at me
How can I ever tell you of the friendship that you offer
The deep understanding and love shown by no other?
An old man now with problems that you can't hide
And in your eyes pure love as you wait by my side
For Ruth you kept a special part of your individual way
And memories that you shared with her only she can say.
You leave behind such sorrow now it's time to go
Who now listens and understands? How I miss you so.
If I could just kiss again your soft brown head
Tears – they fill my eye
You'd have licked them all away
I wish time back I could buy.

Sam

(18.08.03 – 15.05.14)

I miss him not being there, I miss him at the door
I miss his loving kisses; I miss his friendly paw
I miss him at eight when he asked for his chew
I miss not sharing news be it old or new
I miss his friendly smile in his own special way
I miss him not being there every minute of the day

I miss you when I return after a long hard day
I miss your warm greeting and all you had to say
I miss your head so soft against my hand
I miss our long walks across soil and sand
I miss not seeing you with your favourite teddy bear
I even miss your toys you had out everywhere!
I miss you listening carefully, your understanding nudge
I miss my good friend who'd never hold a grudge
I miss you sitting waiting on the fifth stair
And when I cross the landing, I miss not seeing you there

Your individual ways so special to you
No one would believe the things that you'd do
You were never really old; you ran and played each day
So loving and gentle, full of empathy
It's now very quiet although I still talk to you
It's a habit I guess that I'll continue to do

The house is still and silent, just me to walk the floors
I hear a familiar sound, I turn, but it's just my feet, no paws
Now I'm left with emptiness, the rooms still full of you
Everywhere I look and in everything I do
A feeling uncontrollable as tears will randomly fall

I miss you not being with me
I miss you
That is all.

Lightning Source UK Ltd.
Milton Keynes UK
UKHW021318040721
386530UK00007B/123